Mary Pix

Ibrahim, the Thirteenth Emperour of the Turks

A Tragedy

Mary Pix

Ibrahim, the Thirteenth Emperour of the Turks
A Tragedy

ISBN/EAN: 9783337294441

Printed in Europe, USA, Canada, Australia, Japan

Cover: Foto ©Thomas Meinert / pixelio.de

More available books at **www.hansebooks.com**

IBRAHIM,

THE

Thirteenth Emperour

OF THE

TURKS:

A

TRAGEDY.

As it is Acted

BY HIS

MAJESTIES SERVANTS.

By Mrs *Mary Pix.*

LONDON,

Printed for *John Harding* , at the *Bible* and *Anchor* in
Newport-ſtreet, and *Richard Wilkin*, at the *King's-Head*
in St. *Paul's* Church-Yard, 1696.

To the Honourable

RICHARD MINCHALL,
of *Bourton*, Efq;.

SIR,

THat fweetnefs of temper I have had the Happinefs to difcover in the honour of your Company in the firft place, and your favourable Opinion of my Play in the next, gives me Incouragement to claim your Prote-ction.

I am often told , and always pleafed when I hear it, that the Works not mine ; but oh I fear your Clofet view will too foon find out the Wo-man , the imperfect Woman there. The ftory was true, and the action gave it Life ; for I fhou'd be very rude not to own each maintain'd their Character beyond my hopes. Then that pretty Ornament, the ingenious Dialogue, thefe might divert you at the Theatre, but thefe avail not me ; the reading may prove tirefome as a dull repeated tale : Yet I have ftill recourfe to what I mention'd firft, your good nature, that I hope

will

will pardon and accept it. I only wiſh my ſelf
Miſtreſs of Eloquence, Rhetorick, all the Perfecti-
ons of the Pen, that I might worthily entertain
Mr. *Minchall.*

Your Noble Family has been long the Glory
of my Native Country, and you are what I think
no other Nation equals, a true Engliſh Gentle-
man, kind to the diſtreſſed, a Friend to all. I
dare not proceed----my Weakneſs wou'd too plain-
ly appear in aiming at a Character which I can
never reach : Therefore, I conclude, once more
aſking your Pardon, and leave to ſubſcribe my
ſelf,

SIR,

Your moſt humble

and Obliged Servant,

Mary Pix.

THE
PREFACE.

I Did not intend to have troubl'd the Reader with any thing of a Preface ; for I am very senfible thofe that will be fo unkind to Criticize upon what falls from a Womans Pen, may foon find more faults than I am ever able to anfwer. But there happens fo grofs a miftake, in calling it Ibrahim, the Thirteenth &c. that I cannot help taking notice of it. I read fome years ago, at a Relations Houfe in the Country, Sir Paul Ricaut's Continuation of the Turkifh Hiftory ; I was pleas'd with the ftory and ventur'd to write upon it, but trufted too far to my Memory ; for I never faw the Book afterwards till the Play was Printed, and then I found Ibrahim was the Twelfth Emperour. I beg Pardon for the miftake, and hope the Good-Natur'd World will excufe that and what elfe is amifs, in a thing only defign'd for their Diverfion.

PRO-

PROLOGUE

Spoken by Mrs. *Cross.*

I'M hither sent, but Heaven knows what to say,
Or how t' excuse a dull Heroick Play ;
Here's nor poignant Repartee, nor taking Raillery,
No Feast for Critick Pit, or Graduate Gallery.
No Beau, who in his very affected Dress,
Does all the Nonsense of his Character express ;
This Play on solid History depends,
Old fashion'd stuff, true Love, and faithful Friends.
The Pit our Author dreads as too severe ;
The ablest Writers scarce find Mercy there ;
Her only hopes in yonder brightness lies,
If we read praise in those Commanding Eyes :
What rude Blustering Critique then will dare
To find a fault, or contradict the Fair ?
This humble Offering at your Feet she lays,
Nor wishes she to live without your Praise :
Strict Rules of Honour still she kept in view,
And always when she wrote, she thought on you.
Then Ladies own it, let not Detracters say,
You'll not protect one harmless, modest Play.
The Hero to our Sex is still inclin'd,
Securing you, we're sure of all Mankind.
If in that charming Circle you will oft appear,
An Empty House we shan't have cause to fear.

Actors.

Actors Names.

Sultan *Ibrahim*,   Mr. *Verbruggen*.
Azema, Grand Vifier,   Mr. *Difney*.
The *Mufti*,   Mr. *Simpfon*.
Muftapha, Aga of the *Janizaries*,   Mr. *Mills*
Amurat his Son, General of the Emperours Forces, } Mr. *Powel*, Junior.
Solyman, his Friend,   Mr. *Harland*.
Achmet, Chief of the Eunuchs.   Mrs. *Verbruggen*.
Several Officers belonging to the Court
Morena, the *Mufti*'s Daughter, beloved by *Amurat*, } Mrs. *Rogers*.
Sheker Para, Favourite Miftrefs to *Ibrahim*, } Mrs. *Knight*.
Zada, *Morena*'s Chief Slave,   Mrs. *Mills*
Mirva, *Sheker Para*'s Chief Slave   Mrs. *Cole*.
Guards and Attendants.

IBRA-

IBRAHIM

THE

Thirteenth Emperour of the *Turks*.

ACT I.

At a diftance : The Mufti *and* Muftapha *appear.*

Near the Audience Achmet *and feveral Eunuchs Enter.*

Ach. HAfte each Attendant to perform his feveral charge
With ftricteft diligence, and moft obfervant care ;
Burn the *Sabæan* Gums, and all thofe rich Perfumes
Where our great Mafter paffes, till every Room
Smell fweet as Altars laden with Incenfe
To the Heathen Gods, fpread the gay *Perfian* Carpets
For his Royal Feet, and you to the Apartments fly
Of thofe Incloifter'd Virgin Rofes, the felect and chofen
Beauties of the habitable World, bid 'em prepare,
Quick let 'em in all their brighteft glories be array'd,
For their Sun, the Mighty *Ibrahim* approaches.
　　　　　　　[*Exit* Achmet, *the Eunuchs follow.*
　　　　The Mufti *and* Muftapha *come forward.*
　Mufti. Now, by our Prophet, what's all this but gaudy Pageantry,
Ill acted Scenes of Pomp and fhow, inftead of real greatnefs :
O my Friend it was not thus of old,
The great Forefathers of this degenerate Man,
Inftead of treading on *Perfian* Carpets,
Trod upon the Necks of *Perfian* Kings :
Whilft now (curs'd reverfe of time) foftnefs and eafe,
Flatterers and Women, fill alone our Monarch's Heart ;
Women enough to undo the Univerfal World
Are here maintain'd, whole ufelefs hundreds,
And with fuch a train of Pride and Luxury,
That Eyes before ne'er faw, nor can endlefs words defcribe :

　　　　　　　　B　　　　　　　　　　　Wou'd

Wou'd you believe it? the Vultures deckt in Painted Plumes,
So eager are for their vain trappings,
That foon as a Merchant Ship falutes the Port,
His Goods are feiz'd, and brought to the *Seraglio* -
Without Account, Value, or Juftice, yet at this
The Pander *Vifier* winks, whilft the poor Owner
Waits in vain for Anfwer or Redrefs.

Muft. Moft juft Obferver, as well as Teacher of our Laws,
By me in Friendfhip like a Brother lov'd,
In counfel like a Father honour'd,
That what you have faid is moft undoubted truth,
The Impartial World muft own. But thefe complaints
Alas, avail not, our Lord hates us his faithful Servants,
And whatever we fhou'd offer, wou'd certainly defpife.

Muft. You are too good, my *Muft.* to be a Favourite here,
Though fo long Married to the Royal Sifter of our Emperour;
Nay, in this bafe Court, your Son, the God-like *Amurat,*
But coldly is receiv'd, becaufe his wondrous Youth
Has fo far out-ftrip'd their floathful Age——
O ! Pity ! that the faireft branch of all the Ottoman Race,
Sprung from a Female Root; yet I fwear
Were he Lord of all that our Tyrannick Mafter holds,
I cou'd not efteem him more, or love him better.
Few Kings his Courage e'er obtain'd, or Vertues;
O 'tis Nobler far a Crown to Merit, than a Crown
To wear.

Muft. Happy's my Son in fuch a Patron,
Who never ceafes to oblige; I know your kind Attendance
Now is on his behalf, to fpeak his Actions
In the Sultans Ear, fo as may obtain his Royal favour.

Muft. It is indeed my chief defign——
But oh ! Manly Vertue, Courage unequall'd;
Fortitude, and all thofe Graces that adorn
The glorious *Amurat,* are truths difpleafing
To our *Ibrahim,* whofe foft Soul deftructive
Beauty charms into a fleep too found
For the Report of Noble Deeds to wake.

Muft. The Vifier is the Minion
Hangs the darling of his heart,
And with ill Counfel poyfons
Every defign that tends towards Vertue.

Muft. Then that vile Woman, to whom
He hath given the fweet Name
Of *Sheker Para,* fhe, with the Vifier,
Joins to ruin *Ibrahim*——

Muft. Whilft he, contrary to our Countries Laws,
Expofes her to publick view, lets her converfe.

With Vifier, Bafhaws, or whom fhe pleafes.

Muft. But that I have a Daughter,
Whofe early Vertue and fincere Obedience,
Ties my Soul to dote upon:
I for my Countries fake wou'd Curfe the Sex.

Muft. That Daughter——

Muft. No more, the Emperours Guards appear,
And fee the Vifier, and the Woman at his Elbow.

Enter Ibrahim, *the* Grand Vifier, Sheker Para, Achmet, *and feveral Attendants.*

Ibrab. I fay the Bafhaw's Treafon is plain,
Therefore *Morat,* attend him with the Bow-ftring,
And my fatal Order——that without a murmur
He furrender Life for his Ill-gotten Wealth.
'Tis thine, my faithful, vigilant *Azema.*

Vif. O facred Sir, whofe Juftice is Divine,
And 'twould be Impious to affirm
The Bafhaw of *Damafcus* hath one Grain of Innocence;
Yet let me beg you wou'd hold that bounteous hand,
The only Wealth I covet is to be my Sultans Slave.
Befides, I have many Enemies, and thefe high favours
Will I fear create me more.

Ibrab. Who dares to be thy Enemy? No, Vifier,
Whilft I proteft thee, Kings fhall for thy Friendfhip fue;
And let thy Foes remember what I commanded laft.

Vif. O let me throw my felf beneath your Royal Feet,
And kiffing your honour'd Robes, difclofe
The Adoration that my heart is full of.

Muft. Fawning Sycophant!   [*Afide.*

Ibra. Rife, good *Azema!* no more!

Muft. Great Sir, I have a Suit to you.

Ibra. What is't, my Religious Councellor?

Muft. Not for my felf, but one much more deferving,
Your Godlike General *Amurat,* who brings
Your Conquering Forces back from vanquifht *Babylon,*
Now lies Incamp'd near this Imperial City:
Next Spring, by your Commands, and his defires,
He goes to *Candia,* to punifh that ftubborn Town,
Which dares refift the Ottoman Armies that are Invincible.
By me he humbly prays your Royal Licenfe,
That this Winter he may remain
At his own Palace here in *Conftantinople.*

Ibra. I'll confider his defires——but at this time
Let all, except my Eunuchs, and my *Sheker Para,*
Leave me——   [*Exit &c.*
Come,

Come, my loved *Sheker*, what haſt thou prepar'd
To calm and tune my Soul, which theſe affairs
Have ruffled from its own Sphere of
Eaſe and Pleaſure——

Shek. To charm my Monarch is the only ſtudy and
Buſineſs of your Slave, and to that end,
Twenty fair Virgins, whom yet your Eyes ne'er ſaw,
I have pick'd and choſen from a thouſand,
And ſet in order for your view.

Ibra. Thanks my good Girl, 'tis by theſe obliging turns
That thou ſecur'ſt the heart of *Ibrahim*.
Give me that grateful Miſtreſs,
Who when her Lover, ſated with that high
Luſcious Feaſt, Enjoyment, ſhe for his
Sickly Appetite
Generouſly prepares freſh Viands ;
I but taſt of them, my ſolid part,
My Friendſhip that remains with thee.

Ach. Now let each Ambitious Maid diſcloſe the Gifts
Of Art and Nature, whether in Voice, or
Tuneful Motion the taking beauty lies ;
With Emulation let it be practis'd o'er
To charm the Worlds great Lord.

> *The Scene draws and diſcovers the Ladies ſet in Order for the Sultans
> Choice, who takes out his Handkerchief, and walks round them ;
> whilſt* Sheker Para *talks to* Achmet.

Sheker. How different, *Achmet*, is this from the *European* ſtories ;
I have read there, twenty Heroes for the Ladies
Burn and die, here twenty Ladies for the Hero.

Ach. It ſhows that Mankind maintains his Charter
Better here, yet loſes ſure the ſweetneſs
Of ſubmiſſive love ; ſee, he ſeems fixt.

Shek. No— the Handkerchief is not dropt yet,
And ſhe's left to uſe her own.

Ach. Now 'tis reſolved———

> [*The Sultan drops his Handkerchief, which the Lady falling proſtrate,
> kiſſes, and takes up, and is led off by two Eunuchs ; the Sultan fol-
> lowing, the Scene ſhuts upon the reſt.*

Shek. Oh *Achmet* ! O my faithful Slave !
If e'er thou lov'ſt thy generous Miſtreſs
Who has from nothing raiſed thee
And plac'd thee in the higheſt Orb that thou canſt move
For wanting Manhood, though thy Soul's all God-like,
Yet thou canſt not riſe to greater honours,
Help me now ; thou know'ſt my raging fires
How Paſſion like a Vultur preys upon my heart,
And the hot flames of love drink up my Spirits,

All

All this, I fay, thou know'ft, and yet bringft No
Remedy.

Ach. True, when thefe Convulfive Fits are on ye,
I from your ravings learn you love the General *Amurat,*
Nor have I been unmindful , even of thofe———
Imperfeᣤt hints ;
But the Phyfician that pretends to adminifter a Cure,
Muft each particular of the Diftemper know.

Shek. O ! I have told thee, o'er and o'er..
Repetition wrecks my Soul———
Yet thou fhalt hear't again,
Full well thou know'ft the Sultan gives me greater Privilege
Than ever Woman had in the Ottoman Court ;
That has undone me, for there I have feen
This Robber of my reft, this cruel charming *Amurat.*

Ach. Knows he his Happynefs ?

Sheck. Yes, Yes, for I have ftole a thoufand burning Glances,
And fent them to his heart
Befides fweet herbs, and Amorous Flowers
(Thofe Hieroglyphicks, and Emblems of our Countrys love)
In Boxes wrought with gold and fet in Jewels
Of unequall'd value, he hath oft received ;
Yet ftill he Ignorance pretends, nor meets my Eyes
But turns his own another way———
Or elfe looks guilty down.

Ach. What ftoick vertue rules in his cold Icy Veins,
And gives him power to refift thofe Eyes ?
Or has another gain'd his heart ?

Shek. Cou'd I find out that, revenge wou'd take the place
Of Injur'd Love, and I fhou'd weep no more ;
Revenge, fweet Revenge, Injuries, Antidote ,
Wronged Womens darling Joy———
The Emperour thinks perhaps,
Becaufe I fhare him with a hundred Rivals
My Nature's tame. No, No!
We eafily give what we defpife
But fhou'd another be ador'd by my *Amurat*
Whilft negleᣤted I defpair,
How wou'd I wrack her, how glut me
With the ruine of their Loves, and them !

Ach. This I have obferv'd, that fince his Incamping near
He often in difguife repairs to this great Town ;
But whether Ambition or Love bring him, I know
Not, for I cou'd never learn his Counfels.

Shek. That, dear *Achmet,* be thy future care,
And name thy own reward. But how canft thou effeᣤt it,
Hath thy prolifick brain yet laid a form ?

Ach.

Ach. Yes, thus——
You know our Princes for State
Are ftill attended by their Mutes, who
Follow into all their Privacies
As being unable to divulge them ; one of thefe
Is near my Stature.
Him will I draw afide, knock out his brains,
And in his habit watch the Princes Motions.
    Shek. Now ! *Amurat*——Excellent !
The time draws near to quench thefe raging fires,
In full poffeffion of my fierce defires ;
Or elfe the ungrateful object I'll deftroy,
Which rob'd my Nights of reft, my Days of Joy.

ACT II.

Enter Amurat, Solyman.

Soly. THis is not fure that *Amurat*
    Who foremoft fcaled the Walls of *Babylon*,
And cry'd aloud, Come on, who fears to die,
Deferves it——yet at a Letter now paufes,
Stops, turns pale, and feems to grow upon the
Earth he treads.
    Am. Thou art no judge, my Friend, you never loved,
Nor fure none ever loved like me,
If I acquir'd glory, 'twas for *Morena*'s fake
That fhe might not defpife me ——
Nor have I more to do if fhe is loft.
    Soly. You terrify your felf with groundlefs fears,
Nor can I from the *Mufti*'s Letter
Difcern a danger threatning towards your love
    Am. Oh *Solyman* ! forgive the frailty of your Friend,
Forgive the follies that Imperious love creates,
Here the Mufti writes, that on earneft bufinefs
He craves my prefence, if he hath difcover'd
The Adoration that I pay his beauteous Daughter,
And then forbid it, how loft a thing is *Amurat*,
For I know well, though her poor Slave fhou'd fuffer
A thoufand wracks , fhe'd tread the rigid paths of Duty,
And let me die, rather than forfeit her obedience.
    Soly. The Guard our Country lays on that fair charming Sex
Caufes my wonder, how you have lov'd thus long conceal'd.
    Am. Kind Heav'n who faw my faithful fuffering heart,
In pity thus difpofed it, a trufty Slave at the

Tranfporting

Tranſporting hours of ſilent Night ſtill gave
Me admittance
To a Garden, which her Apartment overlook'd,
There, at that awful diſtance, did I Kneel,
Sent up my Vows with ſuch an ardent zeal
Till at length I melted the heart of my fair
Liſtening Goddeſs;
And ſhe from thence, as from an upper Orb of bliſs
Sent down ſweet words, and anſwering ſighs,
The long expected Manna, for which with ſuch
An Eagerneſs,
I had prayed———Ah Souldier! cou'd I impart
But one grain of this fierce paſſion which invades
My Soul, to thee; you no more wou'd wonder
If I almoſt Conquer'd Impoſſibilities to ſee *Morena*
Mark, how the fluſhing joy leaps to my Cheeks,
Oh! if her very name cauſes ſuch boundings in my blood,
What wou'd her ſight, what to preſs her in my Arms,
And taſt her roſy Lips! exceſs of Joy wou'd work
The Effects of grief; and I ſhou'd fall a Victim
At her feet.
    Soly. Where Heaven gives the greateſt hearts
We ſtill the greateſt Paſſions find,
And 'tis the brave alone love moſt and beſt.
    Am. My Dear Indulgent Friend, farewel,
At the uſual Rendezvouz I'll be
Within few hours; and we'll return
Together to the Camp.
    Soly. Proſperity attend your Wiſhes.   [*Exeunt ſeverally.*

Enter the Mufti, *and* Muſtapha, Amurat *meets them attended,*
amongſt his Attendants Achmet.

Muſt. Welcome Noble Youth, you're moſt welcome here,
Nor is your requeſt forgot, though not obtain'd,
For your appearing publickly.
    Am. Where ſhall I pay my duty firſt?
Or which way Kneel? each is a Father,
And each too good for *Amurat.*
    Muſt. Moſt ſure my Son, you never can
Enough acknowledge the bounties
Of this Reverend Man; whoſe early care
Shelter'd thy tender youth———
From the rough Blaſts of Tyranny
And Faction, and by his Eloquence
Still render'd thee as now thou ſtandeſt,
Favourite to the Prince, and People.

                                                                Muſt.

Muſt. My Friends, ye over-rate my Endeavours
To ſerve, and kindly take the will where power is wanting.
No, 'tis not I, 'tis our great Maſter, to whom
Half the Earth bows down their ſervile Necks :
Who, with one Almighty nod, can give a little World
Away, 'tis he ſhou'd *Amurat* reward, and beſtow
A Kingdom, as his Valour due ; yet lovely
Royal Warrior, if I have rightly found
The ſecret of thy heart, there is a preſent
In my power, which equal to a Crown you'll prize.

Morena *Entering.*

Am. Ha !———

Muſt. Come forth, *Morena*, my Ages Darling,
And my hearts delight ; Joy of my Eyes,
Lov'd object of all my Earthly hopes,
Lend me thy hand, and ſmile upon thy Father
When he gives thee to thy Wiſhes.

Am. Where am I ?
Thou tranſporting Image that dances thus
Before my dazled Eyes, art thou real ?
Oh ! that at the emptying half my Veins,
I were convinc'd this is no Dream.

Muſt. I ſaw your ſecret Love, watch'd the kindling fires,
And bleſt 'em as they ſprang. Had I diſapprov'd
They had been prevented e'er riſen to a mutual flame,
But take her, Son, and Eternal Bleſſings Crown ye both.

Muſt. He is already bleſt, what Monarch wou'd not forego
An univerſal ſway for ſuch a charming Maid ?

Am. Speak Goddeſs, ſpeak ! Angel, ſpeak !
Let your ſweet Voice confirm my Happineſs,
That my beating heart may force its paſſage
Through my Breaſt, and fly to yours !

Mor. O *Amurat* ! ſpare my Tongue and Cheeks
The ſhame of owning what my Soul is full of ;
And by my paſt Love, judge my preſent Joy !

Ach. Aſide. Thy future Miſery I can read.

Am. 'Tis ſo, and I am bleſt above all humane kind :
Reign, reign, ye unenvy'd Monarchs !
Fight for this Dunghil Earth, and let
The blood of thouſand thouſand Wretches,
Whom daily your Ambition Sacrifices,
Lie heavy on your guilty heads,
Whilſt I, bleſt with this fair Heaven of Innocence,
This matchleſs, lovely, charming Creature,
More Worth than *Indies* joyn'd to *Indies* ;
Than all the Sun e'er ſees : am Happier

Than

Mor. Ceafe thefe tranfports, my lov'd Lord,
Leaft fate grow angry at our Joys Excefs,
And Dafh them with Eternal Woes.
  Muft. Make haft, my Son, in your return
To the Camp, for fear the Emperour
Shou'd Difcover our private meeting.
Within few days,
You will return with his Permiffion,
And from my Arms, receive the lov'd *Morena*
Into yours!   [*Exeunt* Mufti *and* Muftapha.
  Am. Oh *Morena!* my *Morena,* Now
Permit me to approach, and fwear
Upon thy fnowy bofom, how much
I love thee, till with warm fighs
I've thaw'd thy Virgin Icy Heart,
And made it burn like mine.
  Mor. What Maid can hear, and be unmov'd,
The Man fhe loves talk at this charming rate;
But Oh! I've read, that Men are all by Nature
Falfe; and this dear pleafing tale of love,
To which I liften with fuch rapture,
Will hereafter be, perhaps, Word for Word
Repeated to another.
  Am. Never, *Morena,* never,
No, here kneeling in the Face of Heaven
I fwear, that though our Law allows Plurality of Wives
And Miftreffes, yet I will never practife it;
May Difhonour wrap my head with fhame
Inftead of Laurels; may I be beaten
Through the Army I command, and branded for a Coward,
When I admit another Love into my Bed or Bofom;
Let our great Mafter be Spectator of my Infamy,
And after that let me live.
  Mor. Hold, my dear Lord, fain wou'd I fay fomething too
To anfwer all this wondrous love,
Were there a Man Valiant, good like my *Amurat,*
And greater than our mighty Sultan, yet wou'd I
Be torn in thoufand pieces, rather than
Break my Plighted Faith.
  Am. No more my Life, what need of Oaths
When Love Cements our Hearts.
O! let me taft a parting Kifs,
The fweet memory of which
Will wing my fwift return.
  Mor. What mean thefe tremblings here?
Why come thefe fighs uncall'd?
                        C

1

I know—— I think I know
You wonnot break your Vow.
   Am. Shall I swear again,
Never yet closer to thy heart.
By all these Virgin favours, never.
Here I set up my rest, and plant my Endless Joys
On this fair work of Nature;
When thou was't form'd, curious Heaven
Smil'd at the Exact Creation,
And every power was pleas'd. Oh! I am fix'd
For ever, till glory force me from thy Arms,
Then in all the Hazards of tempestuous War,
Thou, *the* Auspicious Star that I'll invoke,
Morena's Name shall guide my Sword to Conquest,
And after those Laborious Toils, eager and longing
For my bliss, the Laurels I have gain'd,
At thy feet I'll lay, Crown'd with thy love
And reigning in thy heart;
Such Raptures my transported Soul will seize,
I here shall find our *Mahomet*'s Paradise.

                                                    [*Exeunt.*

Enter Sheker Para, *and* Mirva *her Slave.*

   Shek. Now is fate at work for me:
Achmet the busy Engine, that darling useful Eunuch,
Close as his genius traces my Hero's secret steps,
And on his Discovery my tortur'd Life depends.
If *Amurat*'s aspiring Soul is only full of Plots
To raise him higher, fixt above the Visiers Power,
And faster in our Empires Honours, I am happy,
For I can further his Ambition; and he in gratitude
Must pay me back with Love, but Oh! I fear
The Victorious Prince full of charms, and blooming youth,
Is rather on the chase of Beauty, then he obtains
The glorious quarry, for though cast in a Cœlestial Mould
How cou'd a Nymph Divine resist him?
   Mir. Madam whilst you talk as if in dreams
Of Heavenly, and Imaginary Beauty,
You forget your own; the Prince I dare
Presume to affirm, fears to offer, doubting,
What he wishes, your Encouragement, and
Dreading our Sultan. You, Madam, know
'Tis safer far Razing Imperial Cities
Than aiming at a Mistress possess'd,
And valu'd by the mighty *Ibrahim*.
   Shek. True, *Mirva*, I have charm'd the wandring God
More variable than the Heathens *Jove*,

He darts but like a falling Star upon
The yielding fair, diſſolves, and then
To her is ſeen no more ; yet his Soul
Is rivetted to mine, hangs on the Muſick
Of my tongue, nay late at my requeſt
For the firſt bloſſoms of the early year, he gave
The obliging donor, the rich Kingdom of *Natolia* :
I look down on the Sultana Queens, deſpiſe
Their Pregnancy, and want of power.

Mir. The Aſtoniſh'd World ſees your amazing height,
And juſtly pays to you their Adoration.

Shek. Ah Flatterer, to what haſt thou betray'd me,
Whilſt my boaſting tongue ſwells with this
Vain ſtory ; my trembling fooliſh loving heart
Beats a ſad Alarm, and preſages all my hopes deſtroyed.

Enter Achmet, in a Mutes Habit.
Ha ! *Achmet,* thy dreſs, thy looks, thy haſt,
Diſcover thy Faith and Diligence——Oh
Quickly eaſe my tortur'd Soul !

Ach. Madam, your laſt and Chief deſire was
To ſee the Prince : if that's Effeded
You muſt not ſtay to hear what I have learnt ;
He paſſes this moment through the remoteſt Gallery
That leads towards the *Boſphorus,* there
I ſuppoſe his Galley waits him, this Key
Shortens your walk, and you may
Meet him in the open ſpace.

Shek. Fly *Achmet,* to my Cabinet, and ſhift thee there
Then wait till my return———
I dare not ask thee——is he a Lover ?

Ach. Madam, he is ; if you ſtay to hear more
You cannot ſee him.

Shek. Yes, I will ſee him ; though ten thouſand's ruine
Hung upon the fatal Interview ! [*Exit.*

The Scene changes to the proſpeǔ of the Sea.
Enter Amurat *Mufled in his Robe.*
Am. to one Attend. See here abouts for *Solyman.* [Sheker Para, *meets him.*
Curſt accident——hcw ſhall I avoid her.

Shek. Ha ! *Mirva* ? is not that our Cœlebrated General ?

Mir. Doubtleſs, Madam, his very motion ſhews him
He cannot ſhroud his Glories.

Am. Excuſe me Ladies ; a buſineſs
Relating only to my ſelf, call'd me for ſome
Moments hither, without our Lords Permiſſion.

Shek. And is this the way we receive our Conquerours ?

Old *Rome* granted Ovations Triumphs
To such exalted Vertue, drawn in the gaudy Chariot
The Noble warriors march'd a long, kindling
In the bright gazing Virgins loves soft fires,
And in the wandring youths Wars fierce
Martial Heats, if through our crowded streets
Mounted high on Persian ruines,
Succesful *Amurat* were to pass (Pardon
My blushes) when I say I think not *Rome*'s
Fam'd *Cæsar*, or her darling *Pompey*, cou'd
Be more admir'd, esteem'd, or lov'd.

   Am. When a Lady praises, I am Dumb.
Shou'd a Man say this, I must call it
Flattery, and I'll resent it.

   Shek. Fames Trumpet blows aloud, I
Catch but the Echo, and repeat it faintly,
Yet I cou'd wish my self an Emulator
In your glory, a Man, your Companion
In the War, for something I wou'd do
To gain your Friendship ; prevent
The lifted Arm of fate, and in my Breast
Receive some wound design'd for you.

   Am. War, with its rough Idea, ought not Madam,
To Disturb your gentler mind, by varying
Nature order'd the sweet mansion of love
And soft desires.

   Shek. But Almighty Nature sometimes fills
Our Souls with both: as I Ambitious
Look up to War, so you methinks,
Too Godlike Hero, might look down to love.

   Am. 'Tis looking upwards, Madam, surely,
When we think of love ; for beauty
The resemblance bears of Heaven,
Love is a pleasing Theme, but I must
Indulge my Ears no longer, least
I forget my Duty, which in my swift
Return's exprest.

   Shek. Fly not with such unwelcome hast.
If you are pleased with any thing
That I can say, I'll take care for
Your excuse, or stay.

   Am. Madam, I have left the Army without
Their necessary Orders, I cannot now
Accept your offer'd favour.

   Shek. Let Confusion be Instead of Order
If your heart's like mine ; for mine is all
Tumultuous, Oh General !.

Awe me not with thy blufhes,
For I have lov'd thee long———You
Perhaps defpife the Jewel, becaufe 'tis offer'd,
But know Vifier Bafhaws, the greateft
Of our Port, in vain have beg'd a fmile.

Am. To the greateft in the Port, and World;
Your fmiles are due, and I injure him
When I hear this. Farewel.   [*Exit.*

Shek. Gone! O Devil!
Keep down, thou fwelling Heart!
Or higher rife, that I may tear
Thee with my teeth! *Mirva*!
Break all the flattering Mirrors!
Let me ne'er behold this rejected Face again!
Have I feen Scepter'd Slaves kneeling
At my feet, forgetting they were Kings,
Forgetful of their Gods, calling alone on me;
Paffing whole days and hours as if meafur'd
With a Moments Sand, and now refus'd
By a Curft Beardlefs Boy! my Arms too
Open'd, all my Charms laid forth! (for
The Joys of Love are double, when our
Sex defires) heedlefs and cold he flew
From my Embrace; fwift as I will do
To form his ruine———*Achmet*! I come!
'Tis he muft raife this raging Tempeft higher,
Though cold to me, his Bofom's fure on fire.   [*Exeunt.*

ACT III.

Enter Sheker Para, *followed by* Achmet.

Shek. ENough, Oh *Achmet*!——Hold! for I can bear no more,
And yet the Inquifitive Soul, fet on mifchief,
And bent for ruine, hangs on the fatal ftory,
Though every Period gives me Death.
——Was my Curft Rival Fair?
For of her Beauty, you have nothing faid;
Or elfe I left that part unheeded.

Achm. Fair!——not opening Flowers,
Not the firft ftreaks of rifing Day,
Not Painted Angels are half fo Charming!
Eternal fmiles ftill Grace her Cheeks,
And Majefty her Eyes; a Thrilling Mufick

Is in her Voice ; which touches every vital,
And teaches hearts to dance.

Shek. I have it now ! Her Beauty then be her deſtruction ;
But—Great Talkers ſeldom Act, and mighty words
Are mighty nothings; like the Crackling Thunder,
Which makes Women fear but ſeldom harms :
'Tis the thinking Mind that in her own dark Cell
Revolves, and then performs——
Where's the Sultan and the Viſier ?

Achm. The Sultan's retir'd to his Repoſe ;
The Viſier in his Apartment alone.

Shek. Faithful *Achmet* ! take this Jewel——
And think thy wretched Miſtreſs loves thee,
Though her thoughts are now too full.
To Expreſs it——
Thrown, like a neglected Flower from the Boſom,
Where I wou'd have flouriſhed,
How quickly ſhall I fade ! Yet——
With the Firſt Angels Expell'd I'll try
To draw *Morena* down, that Saint above,
To my black Region of Deſpair !

Achm. Though ſhe has Charms, wou'd ſtop the fury
Of our Barbarous Troops, when they take
A Chriſtian Town ; yet I cou'd flea her lovely Face
With my Keen Dagger ; extinguiſh thoſe
Shining Lights, her Eyes, to Revenge my Patroneſs !

Shek. Yes, Rival ! ——
Or thy Vow'd Conſtancy, I'll tryal make ;
And thou ſhalt ſuffer, for thy Lovers ſake !
If *Amurat* Thou Loveſt to that degree,
My ſweet Revenge will then compleated be ;
For I'll take care to ſpoil the Worſhipt Shrine,
And tear Thy Heart, as thou haſt tortur'd mine !

The Viſier ſitting by a Table, whereon lie Books of Account, Riſes.
Viſ. What is't to amaſs theſe mighty ſums of Wealth,
To be daily crowded with preſents from *European* Kings,
To Command on Land, and Sea, next to our Lord,
Whilſt yet I ſtand unſafe between theſe Rocks
Of Regulating the People, and a Tyrant Prince !
All thoſe bitter curſes which they dare not ſhoot
At *Ibrahim*, fall thick on me, the *Mufti*,
And *Muſtapha*, that *Aga* of the *Janizaries*,
Are two I hate, the firſt, becauſe
Like other Churchmen, inſtead of Prayers,
He ſtudies Politicks ; in vain they Preach
Humility, and teach us to look up for Crowns above :

When

When we behold them fix'd on thefe below,
And more ambitious than the Kings that wear 'em.
The Aga's Son, that hot-brain'd Youth, *Amurat*,
Who dares fight, and therefore fcorns to bow,
Or feek my favour : Thefe have cenfur'd me,
And on thefe I'll be reveng'd——

Enter Sheker Para *behind him.*

Shek. On whom is't thou art ftudying revenge,
Old Statefman ! would'ft thou have it bitter,
Deep and fecure ; take a Woman with thee !
——Or Bloody, as thy remorfelefs Heart can frame,
Still take a Woman's Counfel ! But——
Say, *Azem*, who is mark'd for Vengeance ?
Vif. To you, I think, I may difclofe——For
All your Foes are mine, and mine are yours——
The *Mufti* and *Muftapha* look awry on our Actions,
Sowing Sedition inftead of wholfome Doctrine.
Shek. By Heaven ! The very fame thefe are,
Thofe I wou'd deftroy——And for that purpofe
Sought you now——I've laid a Train——
Which wants but your affiftance to o'erthrow 'em all.
Vif. Name it, fair Charmer, quickly !
Shek. This old Crafty Prieft conceals a Daughter,
Whofe Beauty, I am told, without the help of Flattery,
(Excels her Sex) to *Ibrahim.*
The Charming wonders I'll relate !
And fet his Amorous Soul on Fire.
Vif. Hold Madam ! have you confider'd what you fay ?
——Is this the vow'd Revenge——to make
His Daughter a Sultana Queen ?
Shek. Short Sighted Politician !——
Had he defign'd her for our Lord, why was fhe
Thus clofe conceal'd ? Befides ; I know
The Mufti hates our Licentious Emperour ; his late
Attempt upon the Relict of *Morat* ;
His defpifing all his Queens when once enjoy'd ;
Three Sons already blefs the Imperial Line,
And make fucceffion fure. Therefore
Shou'd her Womb prove fertil ; the Royal Innocents
Are only Born for Sacrifice——thefe Reafons
Weigh'd as foon he'd give his Daughter
To a Brothel, as the Sultans Arms.
Vif. I yield.——Let it but provoke him, or his Friends
To Murmur, and I'll ftrangle Rebellion in their Throats.
Shek. Come with me, and attend the Sultan ;

As we go, I'll inſtruct you, how
This Contrivance reaches the Aga, and his Son,
Breaking all their Meaſures.

 Viſ. I wait upon you.   [*Exeunt.*

      [*The Sultan upon a Couch,* Achmet *by him.*

 Ibra. From troubl'd Dreams my tortur'd Fancy Starts:
Sleep, meant nature's refreſhing Friend, ſits heavy
On my Soul, as Death her moſt inveterate Foe.
Achmet! my faithful Boy! art thou there!   [*Sees* Achmet.
 Achm. Dread Sir the Muſick waits without!
Prepar'd by the Italian Maſters——Their Melody
May Chaſe theſe Melancholy Fumes away.
 Ibr. Admit 'em.

A SONG.

*I*Mperial Sultan, Hail,
 To whom Great Kingdoms bow,
Whoſe Vaſt Dominion ſhall prevail
 O'er all below,
Commanding Woman here
An Humble Vaſſal ſhall appear,
No thunder in her Voice we prize,
Or Lightning in her Eyes,
When our Terreſtrial God draws near.
Under our Prophets Influ'nce Live,
 While wondring Nations view
The deeds your Conquering Armies do
And Chriſtians to be made your ſubjects ſtrive.

A Dialogue Song.

Suppos'd to be between an Eunuch Boy and a Virgin.

Made for *Boyn* and Mrs. *Croſſe.*

Written by *Mr.* D' URFEY.

She *F*L *Y from my Sight, fly far away;*
   My Scorn thou'lt only purchaſe by thy Stay,
   Away, Fond Fool, away.
He *Dear Angel no,——no no no no,*
   Here on this Place I'll rooted grow.
   Thoſe Pretty Eyes have Charm'd me ſo:
   I cannot Stir, I cannot go.

She

She	*Thou Silly Creature, be advis'd*
	And do not stay to be despis'd ;
	By all my Actions thou may'st see
	My Heart can spare no room for thee.
He	*Why do'st thou hate me, Ah confess :*
	Thou sweet disposer of my Joys?
She	*The Reason is, I only guess,*
	By something in thy Face and Voice,
	That thou art not made like other Boys.
He	*Why, I can Kiss, and I can Play,*
	And tell a Thousand Pretty Tales ;
	And I can Sing the livelong Day ;
	If any other Talent fails.
She	*Boast not thy Musick, for I fear*
	That Singing Gift has cost thee dear,
	Each warbling Linnet on the Tree
	Has far a Better Fate than thee,
	For they Lifes happy pleasures prove,
	As they can Sing, so they can Love.

Chorus of Both.

He	*Why so can I :*
She	*No no, poor Boy.*
He	*And tast Love's Joy.*
She	*No no, poor Boy.*
He	*Why cannot I ?*
She	*Pish pish——Oh Fye!*
He	*Pray do but try ?*
She	*No no, not I.*
He	*I know, I know, no reason why ?*
She	*You know, you know, you know You lye.*

Enter Visier *and* Shekar Para.

Shekar *kneeling.* —Health to the Ruler of the World ;
Success attend his Armies : whilst
His own happy Hours, with surprizing Joys
Are ever Crown'd ; and long Life proves
A Seraphick Cordial, without Alloy or Dregs.

Visier. May all the mighty *Ibrahims,* and
Our Prophet's Foes fall beneath his Feet ;
And every Slave bear a Heart——
Obedient, and Fond as mine.

Sult. As Heaven hath given me a Despotick
And unbounded Power : so shall my Pleasures be.
But oh! the Earth's too little ; and its Pleasures
Too few ! I cannot keep my mind

D

In a continued Frame of Joy ; tho' the Slaves
That ferve me, vie with the Stars for number!
Nay, tho' you, my Charming Miftrefs,
Whofe very conceptions, like your Wit, Divine,
And like your Beauty pleafing : tho' you, I fay,
Set your Invention on the Wrack, for my Diverfion ;
Yet ftill, to day's like yefterday : to morrow like to day.
And tho' my Paths lie all thro' Paradife :
Yet being ftill the felf-fame Road, I grow uneafie.
    Shek. Alas ! Dread Sir ! we've been miftaken ;
In vain we've fearch'd *Perfia*, and
Armenia, and Ranfack'd *Greece* in vain ;
Whilft within your own Royal Gates
Of this *Seraglio*, lives a *Helene*, whofe
Lovely Face ftrikes Envy dumb.
Late I faw her at the Baths ;
But, Heavens, fuch a Creature.
My aftonifh'd Eyes ne're view'd before.
A Skin, clear as the upper Region,
Where Thickening Clouds can never mount:
And ftrow'd with Blufhes, like the glorious fpace
Of Summer's fetting Suns.
Her large Black Eyes fhot Rays intermingl'd   *The Sultan Rifes haftily.*
With becoming Pride, and taking Sweetnefs.
    Sult. ——Here in our Pallace——impoffible
       ——Of what Name? what Quality?
    Shek. *Morena*, only Daughter to the *Mufti*——But,
For what caufe conceal'd I am ignorant.
    Vif. Had I Daughter, or Wife, whofe Attractions
Cou'd draw the *Sultan*'s Eyes ; how quickly fhou'd fhe be, offer'd!
    Sult. By Heaven ! I'll fee her, fee her this very moment ;
And if fhe anfwers your Defcription,
She's mine ; firft with Prayers, and Mildnefs
We'll proceed ; but, if the furly Fool denies ;
He foon fhall find that Prayers are
Needlefs, when Power is Infinite.
    Vif. I humbly beg to be excus'd, becaufe
The *Mufti* bears me mortal hate,
    Sult. Come thou, my *Shekar*, *Para*,
Thy Eloquence may be ufeful,
Tho' few perfwafions fure will
Prevail, to make a Woman Reign.   *Exeunt Attended.*
          The Scene changes to the Mufti's *Apartment :*
              He fits Reading.
          A Servant Enters haftily.
    Serv. Oh ! Sir —I faw the *Sultan* pafs the Long Gallery,
That parts the Old *Seraglio* from the New ;   And

And bend his steps directly hither—He's 'een at my Heels!
Muft. What can this visit mean?
But I am arm'd with Innocence
And therefore know no fear.

Enter Ibrahim, Sheker Para Achmet, *and several Attendants.*

Muft. Sacred Sir! I am amazed——
At these unwonted Honours; and if I fail
In the expressions of my Joy; let my
Confusion plead my excuse.
Ibr. 'Tis all well, and the visit meant in kindness:
I think when last I saw you,
You asked for *Amurat's* appearance at our Port—
Selim go thou to the Imperial Camp
And tell the Youth he shall be Welcome
There as soon as he pleases.
Muft. Let me kiss your Sacred Robe,
In thankfulness. —Oh! mighty *Sultan,*
Who daigns thus to oblige his Vassals.
Ibr. Mufti—I hear thou hast a Daughter——
Why doft thou start, Old Man? ——
If Fame may be believed thou need'st not shame
To own the Beautious Maid——
Send for her hither, for I will see her.
Muft. Oh! Pardon me Emperour, the Girl is most unfit
For you to see, Bred up in Cells, and Grotto's:
Tho' so near a Court, wholly unacquainted with its Glories.
Heaven not Blessing me with a Male, I have try'd
To mend the Sex; and she, instead of (coining looks)
And learning little Arts to please, hath Read
Philosophy, History, those rough Studies:
And will appear like a neglected Villager.
To those bright Beauties that attend the happy Port.
Ibr. Ha! Is this our entertainment——to be deny'd
What we desire! go some of you and fetch the Maid.
Exeunt two Eunuchs.
Muft. Tho' you are Lord of all, and may without controul
Command, yet Emperor, Remember,
My Daughter is no Slave, and our holy Law
Forbids that you should force the free,
Therefore if the unhappy Girl shou'd please,
And then refuse the offered Greatness; our Prophets Curse
Falls heavy, if you proceed to Violation.

Enter Morena *Veil'd.*

Muft. Kneel Daughter, to the Commander of the World.
Ibr. Take off her Veil——by Heavens——

A

Shekar Para, to prepare for the Excelling honours
I defign her; *Mufti*, come you with me, and let us
Farther confult of this Important bufinefs.

Exeunt the Sultan Mufti *and* Eunuchs : *except* Achmet.

Shek. Hail! Happy Maid! whom *Fate* has bleft ;
Whofe Illuftrious Eyes have caught
The Monarch of the Earth, *Ibrahim!*
Companion to the Sun, and Brother to the Stars!
His Sacred prefence ftrikes an univerfal aw ;
And next to the Immortals he is worfhipt here.
What a long Train of glory is opening to your view,
Mounting on fhining Thrones your beauties Merit!
Whilft thoufand ready flaves ftand watching
The Motions of your eyes, and e're you form
Your breath into command, 'tis done.

Mor. Ceafe Madam, you ufe your Eloquence in vain,
Menaces, Prayers, and Promifes are loft on me.
Already I have Slaves, who wait on my defires,
And fulfil whatever I command : more is but fuperfluous ;
No Crown I covet, but that which honour gives ;
And my Ambition terminates in the contented paths
Of virtue. All your Efforts to alter me,
Like waves againft a Rock, will dafh themfelves,
But ftir not my Foundation.

Shek. Why do ye view me with that haughty
Regardlefs Air, as if I were your Enemy ?
When I fo long to be your Friend,

Mor. Oh! miftake me not, —— If my looks
Carry a difdain, 'tis on the Crowns you offer ;
Not on you, Alas! you only can be my Friend ;
And divert the Emperour from the purfuit
Of this fhort-liv'd paffion; you do not know
The fecret pleafing caufe that will, I am fure,
Infpire me rather to dye than yield.

Shek (afide) Too well I know it!
—— If I cou'd affift, tho' your defires are ftrange,
Yet, you have fomething fo ingaging,
If I cou'd, I fay, I wou'd.

Mor. Oh! 'tis greatly in your power——
Tell the *Sultan* you have difcovered,

'As

As you eafily may a thoufand Imperfections
That I am fickly, peevifh, ill Bred, and
Of a hateful difpofition.———
    Shek. I cannot fo deny your Excellencies ;
But I will do my beft, that you fhall hear of this no more.
    Mor. And now, fair *Oratrix*,
Who plead'ft too well for fuch a caufe ;
Apply thy Rhetorick to *Ibrahim* ;
And defend *Morena's* Life and Honour.
    Shek. Reft fecur'd, I am wholly yours,
Retire fair Innocence, for I fee
This furprize has difcompofed ye.
The Lively Red forfakes the charming Circle
Of your cheeks, and fainting palenefs takes its place :
Retire, and let this Rancontre never trouble your repofe.   *Exit.* *Morena]*

Poor eafy Fool ! blufh *Amurat*
At thy ill choice ! — take me
For her Friend ! yes to her deftruction
I'll prove a conftant one.
    Achmet ! ———
    Ach. Madam.
    Shek. I go to feek the *Sultan*, chufe fome
Of the Eunuchs you command, and fetch
Morena to him, if you meet refiftance,
Bring her by force : I faw *Ibrahim*
Faften his Eyes upon her, and I know
The prefent will be welcome, now if delay
The roving defires of that unftedfaft Prince
May fix elfewhere, and my defigns be loft ;
Make hafte, her Father is not yet returned,
And you may do it with much eafe
    Ach. It fhall be done e're you have time to think the confequence.   *Exit*
    Shek. Revenge ! how quick and lively are thy Joys ?
Love is a fweetnefs, that but tafted, cloys ;
Love muft be fondled with a gentle hand
Revenge is God like all, and fhows command.   *Exit*

        The Sultan Enters ; the Vifier following him.

    Sult. VVou'dft thou believe it *Azema* ——
This crabbed Prieft do's in effect
Deny his Daughter ; curfes he denounces
If I compel her will, and feems
To know fhe'll prove unwilling.
    Vif. In this his difloyalty too plain appears
What other Grandee o'th' happy Port
But with open arms wou'd embrace the honour
And lay his Daughter proftrate at your Royal feet.   *Sult.*

Unequall'd Refolution fhe repuls'd
Whatever I cou'd offer, nor wou'd a Diadem,
Or the Crown Imperial tempt her.

Sult. How comes the lovely Maid to bear a Heart
Thus ftubborn! and look fo fweetly mild?

Vif. 'Tis her Father who has transferr'd
His own traiterous Principles to her,
Taught her early Difobedience
(That I live to fpeak it!)
Taught her to abhor your Royal Perfon.

Shek. But your Majefty now may mould her as you pleafe,
Within a moment fhe'll be here;
I took the opportunity of her Fathers abfence,
And order'd *Achmet*, with his Fellows, to bring
Her hither.

Sult. You have done well,
Shall my almighty Will
Which half the Univerfe obeys,
Without difpute be contradicted
By a Woman?

Shek. I hear 'em coming.

Achmet *brings* Morena, *who fpeaks entring.*

Mor. Whither? Ah! Whither?
Do ye drag me, Audacious Slaves
Am I to be thus ufed?

Vif. Madam, filence and awe beft becomes
This place which the dread Majefty of all the World contains,
Nay our Law's fo ftrict
That an outragious Noife near the Sacred prefence
Is punifh'd with immediate Death.

Mor. Death I defpife as I do thee,
Who art not worth my anfwering,
But to mine and my Countreys Lord
I caft me with an obedient heart:
Daign Mighty *Sultan* to hear with Mercy
What your weeping Slave can fay!
Far be it from your humble Handmaid
To refufe the vaft Honour of your offer'd Love
Thro' pride———Oh! no!

Holy

Your royal heart is full of soft humanity :
And God like Juſtice ; you cannot take
Anothers right —— a thouſand willing beauties
VVill with Joy, Embrace thoſe favours
I muſt ever fly——

Ibr. If thou haſt vow'd, I cancel it,
My Subjects are my ſlaves, who er'e
Pretends a right to what I deſire
Is a Traytor, and ſhall ſo be puniſhed
If thus perverſe you muſt be forced
To your own happineſs——

—*Achmet*——

Mor. O ſpare me Emperor ! ſpare me !
And all my future life I'll ſpend
In prayers for *Ibrahim* !
Each morning as I bleſs the riſing day
I'll cry aloud, this id'e ſeen no more,
Had not my God like Maſter heard :
I'll never eat, nor ſleep, nor
Ought of life enjoy, before I have pray'd for
And after praiſed our Lord

Ibr. Achmet—bear her to the royal bed.
Mor. Hold ! yet a moment ——hold !
I have one thing more to ſay
As I have often heard my wretched Father tell
—When fierce *Morat*, your Predeceſſor
Doom'd his brothers, even all the young Princes
Of the Imperial race, to ſuddain death,
They dyed : my Father begged for you :
Begged till he prevail'd : Oh ! if this merit ought
Puniſh my diſobedience with Wracks with Gibbets,
With any thing but loſs of honour !
Tear out my eyes, ſtab, mangle my face ;
Till it grow horrible to Nature
And the amazed world gaze with terror,
Not delight : burn me ! heap torture
Upon torture ! and if I murmur a complaint
Fulfil the bitterſt curſe ——Releaſe,
And bear me to your bed !

Shek. Speak *Viſier*, he ſtands confounded.
Vij. Dread Sir, what ſtops your wiſhes ?
This is nothing but a guſt of Paſſion,
Plain Woman, her will is croſt,

                                                        'And

And so she raves! e're while you mourn'd
Your pleasures were too much alike;
Fate hath now obliged ye:
This beauteous Maid resists: and all
You ever had before, were willing.
  Ibr. And there may be a new unknown delight
To conquer all these struglings,
Something Poignant, that will relish Luxury————
Do as I Commanded————

          1 *of the Eunuchs.*
Wou'd our worshipt Lord free this
Mourning Fair; Id'e search the
Earth's bounds, to find another,
That might please as well.
  Ibr. Taught by my *Slave!*
Take that, presuming fool.   *Stabs him.*
  Mor. Murder, and Rapine!
What a horrid place is here!
My turn is next————   *She catches hold of the Sultans naked Scimiter.*
  Ibr. Let go rash Maid,————
Or I shall hurt thee.
  Mor. Never, never, I'll leap, and
Fix it to my breast, while some kind God
That sees the anguish of my Soul
Shall help my weakness, and send it to my heart!
  Ibr. Some of you unlose her hold————
  Mor. Then thus I quit it.   *Draws it thro' her hands.*
See Emperor, see, are these hands
Fit to clasp thee? judge by this,
My resolution—death hath a
Thousand doors; Sure *Morena*, curst *Morena*
May find out one————
  Ibr. Slaves, why dally ye thus?
By Heaven rage is mixt with love,
And I am all on fire!
Drag her to yond Apartments!
  Mor. Do Tyrant! but 'tis thy last of mischiefs
If thou dost not kill me ————
With dishevell'd hair, torn Robes, and,
These bloody hands, I'll run thro' all thy Guards
And Camp, whilst my just complaints, compel rebellion!
  Vis. Yet here! force her way!
  Mor. I will not stir, fixt upon Earth,
I'll rend obdurate Heaven with piercing
Crys; till I have forced their mercy!
Help! help! open thou Earth to hide me!
Have my woes not weight enough to sink me

                        To

To the Center ? ——at length 'tis come ;
My fpirits are decay'd, Oh *Amurat* !
Where art thou? and where (alas) am I ? *Swcons.*
 Vif. She faints, convey her quickly in,
Your Majefty
Will foon revive her.
 Ibr. Threatning Danger fhall never bar my way,
I'il rufh thro' all, and feize the trembling prey :
Rifle her fweets, till fenfe is fully cloy'd ;
Then take my turn to fcorn what I've enjoy'd.| *Exit.*

ACT IV.

The Muft. *Apartment.*

Enter Muft. *and* Muftap.

Muft. IN vain you footh me with thefe promifes,
I'll tear my facred Veftments ; make bare
My hoary head, and of thefe *Janizaries*
My felf beg prefent Aid, —was there but one
In all this mighty Empire, chaft, and muft
The Licentious Tyrant feize her ?
 Muft. I have not flatter'd ye—the *Janizaries*
As one man, are bent to right your wrongs
A moment's patience—before to morrow's Sun
The *Seraglio*'s forc'd—the Villain Vifier
Torn limb from limb, and the fair unfortunate reftor'd
—Ha—fee where the lovely Mourner comes.

Enter Morena *led by* Achmet, *her hair down,
and much diforder'd in her drefs.*

Ach. The Emperour hath fent your Daughter back,
You muft tutor her better, teach her
A more complying Nature, then
Perhaps he may again receive her.
 Muft. Hence *Pandar !* accurft by Heaven,
Hence ! left (tho' unarm'd) with
My hands I throttle thee, tell
Thy ungrateful Mafter, the faving
Of his life, is well rewarded——
—Tell him——I thank him
And he fhall hear it loud !

E

Exit Achmet.
Mor.

Mor. Oh Sir ! ———
Muft. My poor Girl ! ———
Muft. Ceafe Daughter, ceafe to mourn !
Here are your Friends ——— Friends
That will revenge ye ———
Mor. O violated Honour !
Ruine, Defpair, and Death's my Lot.
Muft. No *Morena*, No, thy Fame's fecur'd !
And fucceeding Ages fhall as a Miracle
Relate thy Conftancy ———yes, injur'd fair,
To the laft Periods of recording Time,
Thy fragrant Name will blefs the World !
Thou, the brighteft Star, that
Ever grac'd the Eaft !
Muft. Anfwer me Prophet, Author of our Law,
What have I done, what horrid crimes committed,
That my aching Eyes are punifh'd
With this doleful fight !
Mor. The Grave will hide me, Sir !
Then you fhall fee this Wretch no more !
Muft. Live, my belov'd unfortunate !
Let death and ruine fall upon
Thofe Feinds that thus have wrong'd thee.
Mor. The Vifier, (my Father)
The Devil-Vifier—when my piercing prayers,
Seem'd to ftop the luftful Sultan :
He blew again the hellifh fire ———
And with his poifonous breath
Urged the fatal act. ———
Muft. We'll drag the Infernal Dog thro' the City
While, in Howling, he furrender his hated life,
Amidft the Injuries and Curfes of the People.
———Dear Friend, hafte and encourage
Thy willing *Janizaries !* lead 'em
To force the Palace
For this accurfed ; I Authoriz'd
By Heaven will fend a Summons to the cruel Emperour;
That he appear before our great Divan
And give account for this unexampl'd
Breach of our holy Law, the forcing of my Daughter.
Amurat, I know will inftantly be here ———
Come in, my Dear, and I will inftruct
Thee to receive him ———
Mor. Oh ! ———
Muft. Why doft thou figh ? my Son knows
The Heroick virtue of thy fpotlefs Soul,

And

(Alas) have been in their.

Enter Amurat, Solyman, *Attendants.*

Soly. A Bridegroom's haste is in your steps,
And in your Eyes a Bridegroom's joy.
Now—we've reach'd the happy place!

Amur. The Sultan received me with a Noble
Condefcenfion, yet *Skeker Para*
That wretch, unworthy of her Sex,
Caft a malicious fmile, and perplex'd me
With words I cannot comprehend,
But why do I employ a thought on the
Vile Creature, when I am fo near
My own Heaven of Perfection?

Enter Mufti.

Behold the bleft Parent of my Love!
At length my Wifhes are compleat,
I come, dear Sir, to pay my thankful
Vows, and receive the only valued Treafure
That the Earth contains——
How fares my Goddefs?

Muft. Oh! wondrous well!
——Young man—I think th'Ambition
That fills thy veins, is only
How to ferve thy Mafter well,
Nor wou'd offer'd Crowns tempt thee,
To a Difloyal act——

Am. My Father! to merit this difcourfe,
What have I done? by all my hopes
I fwear—fhou'd Sultan *Ibrahim*,
Send the Bow-ftring, Now, Now, when
Pleafure beats thick upon my heart,
And the tranfporting Joys of yielding Love
Are in my view; yet on my obedient knees
I'd fall; and whilft my breath cou'd form
It felf to words; Dying blefs the Emperour,
Oh! I know not whether I, the Sultan
Moft Revere, or my *Morena* Love?

Muft. 'Tis well :——fuppofe then

E 2

This

This lov'd *Morena* torn from her
Helpless aged Father's Arms——dragg'd to
The presence of your honour'd Emperour,
Whilst his Cheeks glow with Lust——
His fiery Eyes dart on the frighted Maid
His fatal resolution ——suppose
Her prayers, her tears, her cryes,
Her wounding supplications all in vain,
Her dear hands in the Conflict cut and mangled,
Dying her white Arms in Crimson Gore,
The savage Ravisher twisting his
In the lovely Tresses of her hair,
Tearing it by the smarting Root,
Fixing her by that upon the ground:
Then ——(horrour on horrour!)
On her breathless body perpetrate the fact.
　Am. What alteration's here?
Chilling Tremblings seize throughout,
And leave my heart as cold as Death:
Oh! Sir! why have you spoke this
Horrid supposition, with such an Emphasis?
——Suppose it true——
Not burning Bulls, not breaking Wheels,
Not all the Cruelties, Witty Tormentors!
Cou'd practise with Fire, Water, Steel, or
Poison, wou'd equal half my Wracks.

　　　　　The Scene draws, and discovers Morena
　　　　　　upon the ground disorder'd as before.

　Muft. Cast thy Eyes that way, and there behold
Thy wretched Fate and mine!
　Am. Oh! Friend! Is this the sight
I promis'd——are these my
Expected Joys——my Eyes!
Fix on the Object you have lov'd
Thus tenderly, and weep till you are blind!
Oh! cruel Emperour! have I for this
Thought toil a pleasure? watching
A delight? Held it a crime to groan
When hundred Aching Wounds were dress'd,
Because I had 'em in thy service?——
——And am I thus rewarded?——
　Soly. At this Scene the Souldier leaves my heart
And I feel the Woman in my Eyes!
　Am. Compassion is a grief of little note,

But I have Woes that tear my Lion heart,
And drink the gushing Blood !
——Speak lovely Mourner, speak
To thy kneeling Slave ; Hath Nature
Form'd a Monster, who durst with violence
Approach thy Snowy vertue ? which
I with a Devotion pure as that we pay
To Heaven, have ever worship'd ?
  Mor. Oh Prince ! No Tongue, no Language,
Not severest sorrow, whose broken accents
Were all made up of sighs, that rend the trembling
Heart which form'd 'em, can express *Morena's* sufferings,
Forc'd from my Heaven of Peace and Innocence,
Thro' what various Scenes of Woe I have passed :
Raging Seas, devouring Flames, and Pestilential Fires,
May be the work of chance ; and Nobly born :
But mine's a Fate strips me of all Patience,
Even of the last, and dearest Comfort, Hope.
Oh ! 'tis my Curse that sense remains,
The Dire Vision is ever present with me
On this side ghastly Murder, on that
Rapine dress'd in Pomp, and Power,
Ruinous resistless Power ! my head
Grows giddy with the Loath'd Reflection,
Lead me, my *Zaida,* to Darkness, solid,
Thick, substantial Darkness, where,
Not one Ray of the all-cheering Light
May peep upon me, prepare an Opiate Draught
To lull my sorrows, or some desperate compound
That may turn my brain————
  Zaida. Heaven calm these sad disquiets, and give
The Best of Women Peace————
  Mor. Your Pardon, Reverend Sir, and thine I ask
Thou illustrious Figure of unfeign'd Despair,
I am not used to rage, my Nature ever gentle,
At but the reading of a dismal story,
My Eyes wou'd flow, my Heart wou'd rise,
And sympathetick sorrow reign.
But now I am by wrongs a Fury grown
Holy Prophet, is it a sin to heave these
Bleeding hands to thee, and *Amurat,* for Justice ?
Yes, yes, it is, for Justice leads to sharp revenge
That to horrid Mischiefs—away—away——
Give me Death, Distraction, any thing, but Thought. *Exit.*
  The Scene shuts upon her.

Am.

The World! ———— wilt
Thou not affist me, Friend ?
  Soly. Whilft I wear this——————Nor
Shall I fear to purge the contagious
Veins of Majefty in fuch a caufe.
  Muft. 'Tis not by Raving we accomplifh
Our Defigns; if, for my conftant
Friendfhip, I have ought deferv'd,
In our honourable proceedings you will joyn :
Come with me to your Father, who is now confulting
With the Officers ——there I'll inform ye
Who were the hateful Wretches, that fet
The Sultan on to do this fatal mifchief.
  Am. I go—— *Solyman,* fly to the Camp,
And bring from thence my felect Troops,
I'll take care at Night to give you fafe admittance ;
Oh World ! uncertain always, falfe, and vain,
Thro' mighty Toils our wifhes we obtain,
And hard we ftruggle for the expected gain :
But when in view o'th' end of all our care,
Some awkard Fate hurls back to deep Defpair,
Thus to th'Abyfs, in fight of Heaven, I fall,
And lofe my Love, my Honour, Life and all.   *Exeunt.*

    Enter Ibrahim, *the* Vifier, Sheker Para, Achmet,
      who feems talking to the Sultan.

  Ach. He threatned me with Death,
And faid, he'd tell his Wrongs aloud,
Till Neighbouring Nations heard 'em.
  Ib. Saucy——and Arrogant !
  Skek. How long fhall the Imperial Race;
Whilft the miftaken World deems them
Abfolute, be fubject to the crafty
Priefthood ? ——Do at once,
A juft bold act, and fet by
Your Example the great Succeffors free,
Send the Executing Mutes, and
Strangle this Ambitious *Mufti.*
  Vif. Strangle the *Mufti!* Oh horrour!

                               Ibr.

Ibr. Why thou Viper, whom my breaſt
Has foſter'd, till the rank poyſon——
Hath made me all Infectious——
VVas it not you that urged
The cruel Rape I laſt committed ?
By Heaven ! The only deed that
Ever moved my Soul to a Repentance !
And doſt thou now ſhrink back ? Y.
Thou whoſe face is ſtamp'd ſo plain
VVith Villain, every child may read it,
Canſt thou draw thy Diſtorted features ,
Into a look of pitty ? and, as if Murder
VVere News, cry out, Oh Horror !
I tell thee, Viſier, and mark it well,
Watch the firſt riſing of Rebellion,
For ſhould it grow too high ; thou art
The fitteſt Sacrifice to attone the Popular Fury.

Vif. Sacred Sir, you cannot mean the
Cruel things you ſay——muſt
My Life pay for my ſincere Obedience
To your Royal Will?

Enter one of the Guard,

Guard. A Meſſenger from the Divan
Rudely preſſes to your Preſence.
Ibr. Admit him——

Enter Meſſenger.

Meſſ. Sultan ! ——the Mufti and the
Whole Divan Aſſembled, have ſent me
To thee with the Mufti's Fatfa.
That you inſtantly appear to anſwer
The breach our Holy Law has ſuffered,
In violating *Morena,* A Free-born Maid.
Ibr. Is then the Mufti the Derviſes, and
All the canting Tr together met
Hatching Treaſon, and brooding in
Their lov'd Element Rebellion ?
Now every petty Prieſt ſtruts,
Looks big ; tells a long tale
Of grievances, Models Governments,
and Cenſures Kings——let your
Ring leader know, that I deſpiſe
His Trayterous Summons, and
Trample it beneath my feet——
Yet, Hold——thou art not fit

To bear a Meſſage back from
Ibrahim, who dareſt to bring him
Such a one ; take hence the Villain,
And ſtrangle him immediately.
    Meſſ. Oh ! Mercy ! Mercy !
    Ibr. Away with him !——
Viſier, Double our Guards, and
From the Army draw all, whoſe Loyalty
You think untainted——be Vigilant——
For on thy Life depends thy care——
Weep not, my _Sheker Para_——
We yet ſhall brave this Storm——
By Heaven !——
    I to the Laſt my glory will maintain,
    Or, abſolute I'll be, or, ceaſe to Reign
That eaſie King, whoſe People gives him Law,
Flatters himſelf with Majeſty and awe ;
The Royal Slave the daring rout commands,
And force his Scepter from his feeble Hands.   _Exeunt_

ACT V.

Enter Ibrahim, Viſier, Sheker Para, _Attendants._

    Ibr. W HY Coward doſt thou creep thus near me,
             Still leaving my Orders unperform'd ?
    Viſ. Oh ! Sacred Sir ! The Mutinous _Janizaries_
Bar each Gate o'th' Palace, nor can I
Paſs with Life !

Enter Achmet.

    Ach. Our woes redouble with the coming Night,
The Impetuous _Janizaries_ pour on us
Like a devouring Flood, whilſt your
Faint-hearted Guards ſcarce dare Reſiſt,
Aloud they curſe the _Viſier_, and
Unanimouſly ſwear his ruine.——
    Ibr. Poor trembling Wizard——if thou haſt
Raiſed a Storm beyond thy Magick Power
To lay, it muſt overwhelm thee——
Here——throw to theſe Ravenous Hunters
The Baited Prey ; and let 'em gorge
Their revengefull Maws.

                                     Viſ.

Vif. Hah!

Ibr. Stop his mouth, and bear him off.

Vif. Sultan, *Ibrahim* ——

'uel Lord! Wilt thou not hear me!

Ibr. I, ſtand next the mark of fate!

ſil Councellors the plauſible pretence

f Rebels, colours their Treaſon ——

.t —— 'tis at Soveraign power they aim,

þr will they ceaſe, till they have bath'd

: Royal Gore ; the Victim's ſeiz'd ——

ſuk how the Bloodhounds ring his Death!   *A ſhout without.*

Shek Oh! That I were a Man to face

ſeſe Devils, and ſave my Lord!

Ach. Retire Dear Sir, to ſome more remote

. þartment, whilſt I together draw

þur Eunuchs ; all whom Prayers

ſ Promiſes can engage, to ſave

ſur precious Life, tho' I looſe my own.

Ibr. Faithful *Achmet*! I, who

ſt yeſterday commanded Armies,

ſhoſe numbers outſtript Arithmetick,

ſnd left them unaccountable :

.ave now but one poor truſty ſlave

.n Eunuch, who for his unhappy

ſord, will venture Life! ———   *Exeunt.*

Enter Solyman and Souldiers.

Soly. Where is this Barbarous Prince ———

I warrant Fellow-Souldiers ; ——Hid

The cruel are ſtill Effeminate :

There's ſcarce a Man left, that

Aſſerts his cauſe, ———I'll ſearch him out,

And whilſt my injur'd friend's preventing

The plunder o'th' City ; do a deed,

At which his nicer vertue ſhrinks.   *Exeunt.*

Ibrahim, *and* Sheker Para.

Ibr. Flatterers, that curſe of Courts have ǀ

Ruined me! ———thro' their falſe

Opticks, I view'd my greatneſs ———

And when I thought my ſelf a God ;

Am more wretched than my meaneſt Slave :

Unregarded Now's the Frown, that

Mark't my foe for Slaughter ; or the

Gracious

And I will dye with all my Majesty about me,
——Go wretched Woman——Herd amongst
Thy Sex, and let that protect thee !——
 Shek. I will a while retire ;. watch this fear'd event,
And if you fall ;————boldly come forth and dye.   *Exit.*

Enter Solyman driving in Achmet.

 Soly. *Eunuch* ! *Pandar* ! dar'ſt thou ſtop my way ?
That for thy impudence——that for the poor *Morena* !.
 Ach. O Sultan ! our Prophet guard thee,
I can no more   *Dyes.*
 Ibr. What bold ſlave art thou. who
Throwing off the Sacred ties of Duty,
Allegiance, darſt with offenſive
Arms approach thy lawful Prince !
 Soly. My Prince !.————
Id'e ſooner ſerve a Ruſſian Bear,
Whoſe inhuman paw, when I was
Moſt Aſſiduous, mark'd me ſtill
With Indignation——ſuch a Monſter
So unaccountable art thou !
Oh ! *Ibrahim* ! Didſt thou but hear
Thy long injur'd, and at length revolting
People, how they curſe thee,——what
A dire Catalogue of crimes repeat :
Hadſt thou left one grain of Honour,
Thou wouldſt turn thy wounded ears away !
And beg me uſe my Sword ; but talk no more.
 Ibr. Traytors are ever loud————
And to colour their own deteſted ſin
Rebellion ; with impudence, and calumnies
Beſpatter the Throne, they dare attack.
 Soly. Was there a Slave throughout thy wide
Dominions, whom blind fate had curſed
With Wealth : His forfeit—Head
Pay'd for his crime : Whilſt his extorted
Treaſure fill'd thy coffers, and ſupply'd.
New Luxury. Did vertue Reign in
Any Man, a life Auſtere ; or active Valour
Like our great Progenitors : Strait you,
And your Minions thought, this lookt

With

With a Reflecting Eye on your Debauches:
Difpatch'd the pious Wretch, and fent him
To his Friends above ; then Women
You monopoliz'd ——— let her be Wife
Or Virgin, fair as Heaven, or monftrous as Hell :
Witnefs your *Armenian* Miftrefs ; all ferv'd
As fuel to that confuming fire your Luft ;
Nay, even the Relique of our late glorious
Emperour, was not free from your Attempt,
But that her Lion Refolution made your
Coward Heart fhrink back.
  Ibr. What! ——ho! ——
Is there none to fecure this Traitor ?
  Soly. I tell thee, Loft degenerate King,
There's not a Soul will move a Tongue
Or Finger, in thy Defence ; thou ftandft
Forfook by Heaven, and Human Aid———
Think now upon the fair *Morena*!
And if thy heart of Adamant unmov'd
Cou'd hear an Angel pray ; if the angry Powers
So punifh'd her fpotlefs Innocence : What
Horrours muft remain for thee ; who bend'ft
Beneath the weight of thoufand thoufand Ills ?
  Ibr. Come on, thou Rebel ! ———
No Souldier fure thou art !
Thy Tongue's thy fharpeft Weapon——yet
If thou wer't ; and did thy acts excel the
Foremoft of my Royal Race ; thy Ignoble
Tomb muft blufh to hold thee, the name of Rebel
Wou'd blot out the *Hero*, and leave thy Fame
Deteft'd, to the honeft World ; as thou
Haft Reprefented mine !
  Soly. My injur'd Friend, and that unhappy Beauty
Whom thy Luft haft ruin'd, gives Juftice to
My Javelin's point, and fends it to thy heart !   *Fight.*
  Ibr. T' has reach'd it too, nor am I far from thine.
  Soly. Oh feeble Arm ! Oh *Amurat* !   *Both fall.*
Cou'd I do no more for thee !
  Ibr. I am no longer now the fport of Fate,
This Atom which our unfeen Rulers
Thus alternately have toft, now will reft
For ever ; my firft beft part of Life,
Even all my Youth, to Dungeons, Dark
And Loathfom as my Grave, a jealous
Brother clofe confin'd : then flatter'd
A while with Empire, Commet like,

F 2   I made

I made a glorious dreadful blaze;
Yet thanks to my Niggard Stars, I Preſt
'The golden fruit of Power, and Drank
The very Quinteſcence, the Viſion
Was too full of Rapture long to laſt:
In a moment the gaudy Scene is vaniſh'd,
And to my endleſs Priſon, I in haſte return.   *Dyes.*

     Enter Amurat, *who ſpeaks to his followers Entering.*

   Am. Sheath all your Swords, here
Let Murder ceaſe; and whilſt in ſad complainings
I move my Royal Maſter's heart——
Let no rude breath offend him——
Ha! ſtretch'd on the floor!——
My Friend! haſt thou done this?   *Sees 'em.*
   Soly. To higher Judges I am ſummon'd to appeal,
Where I reward or puniſhment ſhall find
For this act; which exceſſive friendſhip forc'd:
If thou in honour, as in valour ſtill excell'ſt,
Forgive thy over-loving Friend: and with a ſigh
Remember all my faults, and Death.   *Dyes.*
   Am. Ye inauſpicious Planets! which at my birth
Shot your intermingl'd Rays; and on my Infant
Head, dropt the poiſonous Influence:
Oh! that I could curſe ye from your Malignant
Spheres! Was ever ſuch a Wretch as *Amurat*?
My Miſtreſs Raviſh'd,——the cruel Raviſher
My Emperour's dead,
My Friend, the Author; and puniſh'd too with death!

    Enter the Mufti *and* Muſtapha, *and ſeveral Commanders.*

See Fathers, ſee the fatal end of
Our Commotions!
   Muſt. 'Twas Heavens will, and therefore grieve no more;
   Muſt. All Eyes are fixt on you, nor doth the
Empire yield an honour, which you may not claim.
   Am. Oh! miſtake not the heart of *Amurat*!
Think not Ambition led me on! no;
Had not Love forc'd my backward Hand,
This Breaſt had been a Rampart to Guard
The Life of *Ibrahim*; and my Sword
Deſtroy'd even you, my Father, had
Ye attempted it!——On the
Illuſtrious Head of the young *Mahomet*
Let's fix the Imperial Crown! May

                                            It

It be larger, and happier than his
Departed Fathers! and with Hearts,
From whence this Voice proceeds, Ring out
The Acclamation——Long live *Mahomet*
The Fourth! Emperour of the true Believers!
  Omnes. Long live *Mahomet* the Fourth, &c.
Amurat our great Deliverer!
  Muſt. Bear the Body to the Royal Moſque, whilſt I,
With *Muſtapha,* wait on the *Sultana* Queens ;
Diſpel their fears, and cauſe the perturbed State
To reaſſume a Face ſerene.   *Exeunt* Muſt. *and* Muſtaphia.

Enter Sheker, Para.

  Shek. Turn, Traitor, Turn! and here behold
Thy Fate! ——'Twas J diſcloſ'd the
Cloiſter'd Maid, and forc'd her on the King
That good Turn I ow'd for your Diſdain.
Then——If you loved *Morena,* wreak
On me your Vengeance ; and ſtrike
Your Ponyard to my Heart!
  Amur. There are things, which by Antipathy
We hate ; and ſuch wert ever thou.
The contaminated Blood ſhall never
Stain the Sword of *Amurat.*
Live! Deteſted Creature! Loaded
With Shame and Infamy! Be it
Thy Curſe to live! whilſt
Pointing Fingers, and buſie Tongues
Proclaim thee, if thou appear'ſt, hunted
Through the City like a Beaſt of prey ;
And ſhunn'd by all, whoever heard
The Name of Goodneſs!
  Shek. Look back! and ſee! how vain thy Curſes are!
Thus! —I defie thy Malice!   (*Stabs her ſelf.*)
Oh! *Ibrahim!* if in the other World
The faithful *Sheker* can be uſeful:
Lo ſhe comes——Diſdaining Life
When thou art gone!
  Amur. Bear the polluted Wretch away,
Whilſt I ſeek my afflicted Fair :
And recount the Wonders Revenge has done.   *Exeunt.*

Enter Morena
Dreſt in White.

  Mor. Dreſt in theſe Robes of Innocence,
Fain wou'd I believe my Virgin Purity remains ;   But

But oh! Memory the wretched'ft Plague,
Still goads me with the hated Image of my wrong.
My Soul grows weary of its polluted Cage,
And longs to wing the upper Air, where
Uncorrupted Pureneſs dwells.

Enter Zayda.

Come near, my *Zayda*, why doſt thou
Tremble ſo? Oh! hadſt thou known
The Horrours, thy poor Miſtriſs has,
Thou woud'ſt have left to fear!
  Zayd. Who can expreſs the Terrours of this diſmal Night!
The mad *Janizaries* up, and raging for Revenge,
Put private Broils upon the publick ſcore,
Murder and Rapine, with Fury uncontroll'd
Rang through the City, and make the Devaſtation
Horrible, the mangled *Viſier* they have
Piece-meal torn; nor has their Vengeance
Stopt here; The Life of the Empire, the Man
We worſhipt like a God, for whom
We ſtill were taught to pray; even
The mighty *Ibrahim* is no more!
  Mor. Is *Ibrahim* dead?——Oh *Amurat*!
I fear thou haſt gone too far; and left
Our Prophet, ſhou'd puniſh thy Diſloyalty;
I will, of my ſelf, an Offering make!
Morena, the unhappy cauſe of all theſe Woes;
  Morena the Atonement————
Go to my Cloſet; bring from thence
The Golden Bowl——This News
Has much diſorder'd me————
There is in that a ſoveraign Cordial!
Look down ye *Roman* Ladies
Whoſe tracks of Virtue I with care,
Have followed——Behold! a
Turkiſh Maid——who to the laſt,
Your great Example imitates:
Scorns to ſurvive when Honour's loſt!

                                    Exit Zayda.

Enter Zayda with the Bowl.

I know my avenging Friends will inſtantly
Be here gay in their Purple Ruins, thinking to glad
My Soul with the fatal ſtory; but like a ſad Wrecth,
Whoſe loſs is irrepparable, I muſt never aim
At comfort more! Deeply I'll taſte this precious Juice,

                                            And

And feek that found long fleep, where forrow,
Tormenting care thofe reftlefs Anxieties
That keep in Dreams the mind awake, approach no more! *Drinks the Foyfon.*

Enter Amurat.

Amur. Hail my belov'd and charming fair!
Oh! I have bin, where Blood and Defolation Reign'd,
Where horror in a thoufand fhapes appeared:
But 'tis paft: And I am arrived at the defired Land
Of Peace——Thou the Dove-like Emblem, whofe
Long'd for fight Calms the rough Tempefts
Of my Soul, and tunes my Heart to Joy!
  Mor. That thou hadft ftay'd fome moments longer.
  Amur. Why! My lov'd dear one!
  Mor. I fhame to caft my eyes towards thine
Wherewith fuch pleafure I was wont to fteal.
A glance, my Revenge is now compleat;
I know it, and am yet alive————
Lucretia dy'd before!
  Amur. Inhuman fair!
Death in the Perfon of my Friend!
Hath toucht my heart too near;
And now, to crown my mifery,
Cruelly you talk of yours!

Enter the Mufti, Muftapha *and feveral others.*

  Muft. The wrongs that Tyrrannick *Jbrahim*
Had heap'd on the *Sultana* Queens
Caufes 'em joyntly to rejoyce;
They call you their preferver,
And fend by me the Empire's Seal   *To* Amurat.
With the Title of Prime *Vifier*:
Begging you wou'd protect the Infant
King, whom you have fo juftly Rais'd.
  Amur. All Honours, Titles, Glories, at the Feet
Of my Adored I lay, if fhe will blefs me
With the fweets of Love, I am, what
They pleafe, elfe nothing.
  Mor. Can the great *Amurat* fubmit fo low,
To talk of Fruition when 'tis paft,
Or to his Arms receive pollution?
  Amur. Name it no more! The Royal Blood
Of the offender hath cleanfed and wafhed cut
Thy Honours Stains, and white as thy

Rebes

Robes, thy Innocence appears.
Shall I forsake the Christal Fountain,
Because a Rough-hewn Satyr there
Has quencht his Thirst ? No ! The
Spring, thy Virgin Mind was pure !

Mor. Talk on, methinks I taste of Heaven,
To hear thee ! Let thy kind Breath
Proceed : Waft me from one Paradice
To another !

Amur. Distraction seize me ! Either
My sight deceives me ; or my Love
Looks exceeding pale ; she Staggers too !
Help ! Help ! Remorseless Powers drive not
The Wretch you form'd to the Blasphemous
Sins Dispair may utter !

Must. My Daughter ! what hast thou done !

Zayd. Oh ! my unhappy Mistriss !
I fear that fatal Cordial !

Amur. Inveterate Stars ! Now ye've stretcht
Your power to the last degree, and
Ye can curse no more !
Oh ! *Morena* ! more savage——
Than our Lord ! for ever thou
Hast Robb'd my Life of Joy, depriv'd
My Eyes of Happiness ; which, till
They close, must gaze on Thee !
What hath my Love deserv'd for such
A punishment ? *Morena* ! unkind !
Cruel ! unkind !

Mor. My Father ! draw near ; forgive this
First, last act of Disobedience !
You taught me, Sir, that Life no longer
Was a good, then a clear Frame attended it ;
My Dishonour Rings through the Universe —
Pardon my quitting it !———
Now *Amurat* ! To thee—Here will I
Lean a Moment, where I thought to Raign
A whole contented Age——I fear the Cordial
Will prove too strong ! Antidote the Poison,
And let me live !

Amur. Thou shalt live ! since this Barbarous
Climate has wrong'd such worth ;
I'le Raise another Empire large as this,
And fix thee there !———

Mor. Fix me in thy Heart ! more dear to me
Than gaudiest Thrones ! Be that

The

The ſacred Urn, where thy *Morena* reſts ;
Nor ever let the Face of newer brighter
Beauty drive her thence !————
Oh ! Farewel !————   [*Dies.*
  Amur. Oh ! ſpeak ! ſpeak once again !————
Open thoſe roſy Doors ! Dart from
The faireſt Eyes that ever bleſt the World,
One Ray though 'tis a dying one ! ————
Oh ! 'Tis impoſſible ! Is there
A Dungeon, Galley, Bedlam, can
Produce ought ſo miſerable as *Amurat*!
  Muſt. Dead, my lov'd Daughter !————
Angry Prophet ! when will thy vengeance ceaſe !
  Amur. Oh ! never let it ! now let
Earthquakes ſhake the Baſis of this Foundation,
And whirlwinds drive us like duſt about !
  Muſt. Have Patience, Son ! Honour was
The Miſtreſs of thy Youth ! Fair
Morena hath form'd the bright Idea
To the Life, Copy her, and court only Glory.
Now let the great Buſineſs of the Empire
Divert thy Sorrow.?————
  Amur. Ye ſay I am Viſier, Guardian to the
Infant King ; with Power unlimitted
Command a World, almoſt as large as
Alexander's————Oh ! *Morena* ! once my
Living Miſtreſs, now my dead Saint,
My Ever Worſhipt Dear : I do remember
What I promiſed : no Crowns, Lawrels, nor
The greateſt height Ambition raiſes,
Shou'd ever mount me above thy Slave————
Thus——thus I keep my word————   [*Stabs himſelf.*
Slighting all offers here I proſtrate ly ;
No life ſo happy, as with thee to die !
  Muſt. Oh ! fatal deed !
  Muſt. Raſh Act !
  Muſt. Where ſhall I hide me from
This Scene of Woe ! ——No ſorrow
Equals that which to the Dead we pay !
Becauſe there's no Room left for
Hope of Friend !
  Muſt. Let's not through grief neglect the publick care
Since in the change we had ſo large a ſhare ;
On the Empires charge let's our ſad thoughts imploy,
There muſt be room for that, though none for Joy.
                                              [*Exeunt.*

G   EPI-

EPILOGUE.

THE Play is paſt, the danger is to come,
    Criticks, in pity give a gentle doom.
To Conquer thoſe who can their Cauſe maintain
Is Glorious ; here the labour wou'd be vain :
By the great Rules of Honour all Men know
They muſt not Arm on a Defenceleſs Foe.
The Author on her weakneſs, not her ſtrength relies,
And from your Juſtice to your Mercy flies.

FINIS.

Advertiſement.

THE Inhuman Cardinal, or, Innocence betray'd. A Novel, 12.
    Written by Mrs. Pix. Printed for John Harding and Richard
Wilkin.